A GIFT FOR

_____

FROM

_____

DONALD MILLER

JAZZ NOTES

Improvisations on

BLUE LIKE JAZZ

New York Times Bestseller

Published in Nashville, Tennessee, by Thomas Nelson.
Thomas Nelson is a registered trademark of Thomas Nelson, Inc.

Design: Kevin Swanson
Editorial Development: Todd Hafer

Photography: tiburonstudios/istockphoto, Henk Badenhorst/istockphoto, blaneyphoto/istockphoto, Remus Eserblom/istockphoto, Terraxplorer/istockphoto, Charles Noble/istockphoto, Dmitry Volkov/istockphoto, John Anderson/istockphoto, cglow/istockphoto, Kativ/istockphoto, M. Eric Honeycutt/istockphoto

Thomas Nelson, Inc. titles may be purchased in bulk for educational, business, fund-raising, or sales promotional use. For information, please e-mail SpecialMarkets@ThomasNelson.com.

ISBN-10: 1-4041-05158
ISBN-13: 9-7814041-0515-7

Printed in China
08 09 10 11 QW 9 8 7 6 5 4 3 2 1

JAZZ NOTES

NONRELIGIOUS THOUGHTS ON CHRISTIAN SPIRITUALITY

DONALD MILLER

THOMAS NELSON
Since 1798

NASHVILLE DALLAS MEXICO CITY RIO DE JANEIRO BEIJING

I NEVER LIKED JAZZ MUSIC,

BECAUSE JAZZ DOESN'T RESOLVE.

BUT SOMETIMES YOU HAVE TO

WATCH SOMEBODY LOVE SOMETHING

BEFORE YOU CAN LOVE IT YOURSELF.

I USED TO NOT LIKE GOD

BECAUSE GOD DIDN'T RESOLVE.

BUT THAT WAS BEFORE

ANY OF THIS HAPPENED . . .

1 BEGINNINGS

I once listened to an Indian on TV say that God was in the wind and the water, and I wondered at how beautiful that was, because it meant you could swim in Him, or have Him caress your face with a breeze.

I am early in my story, but I believe I will stretch out into eternity, and in heaven I will reflect on my early days, the days when it seemed sometimes like God was down a dirt road, walking toward me. Years ago, He was a swinging speck in the distance. Now He is close enough that I can hear His singing. Soon I will see the lines on His face.

My father left home when I was young, so when I was introduced to the concept of God as Father, I imagined Him as a stiff, oily man who wanted to move into our house and share a bed with my mother. I remember this as a frightful, threatening idea.

We were a poor family who attended a wealthy church, and they told us we were children of God. So I also imagined God as a man who had a lot of money and drove a big car. I felt that God's family was better than mine – that he had a daughter who was a cheerleader and a son who played football.

I was born with a small bladder, so I wet the bed until I was 10. Later, I developed a crush on the homecoming queen. She was kind to me, in a political sort of way, which she probably learned from her father, a bank president.

So, from the beginning, the chasm that separated me from God was as deep as wealth and as wide as fashion.

I have been with my own father only three times, each visit happening in my childhood. He was a basketball coach, and I do not know why he left my mother. I know only that he was tall and handsome and smelled like beer.

It was on his clothes, even on his coarse, uneven face. I don't drink much beer myself, but the depth of that scent has never left me.

My friend Tony the Beat Poet will be drinking a beer when we're at Portland's Horse Brass Pub, and the smell will send me to a pleasant place that exists only in recollections of childhood.

My father was a big man. I think bigger than most. On my second visit with him, he threw a football across a gym, drilling a spiral into the opposite hoop, so hard that it shook the backboard. I studied my father's every action as a work of wonder. I watched as he shaved and brushed his teeth and put on his socks and shoes – all motions that were more muscle than grace. I would stand at his bedroom door, hoping he wouldn't notice my awkward stare. I looked purposefully as he opened a can of beer, the tiny can hiding itself in his big hand, the foam spilling over the rim. His red lips slurping the excess, his tongue probing his mustache. He was a brilliant machine of a thing.

It is not possible to admire a person more than I admired that man. I know, from only three visits, a blend of love and fear that exists only in a boy's notion of his father.

Years passed between his calls. My mother would answer the phone, and I knew by the way she stood silently in the kitchen that it was my father. A few days later, he would visit, always changed in the showing of his age. The new wrinkles, the graying hair, the thick skin around his eyes. He would take my sister and me to his apartment for the weekend.

About the time I entered middle school, the visits stopped, and my father disappeared.

o o o

Today I wonder why God refers to Himself as "Father." In light of the earthly representation of the role, it seems like a marketing mistake. Why would God call Himself a Father when so many fathers abandon their children?

As I child, I found the title Father God to be an ambiguous haze. I understood what a father did about as well as I understood the tasks of a shepherd. All of the vocabulary about God seemed to come from ancient history – before video games, the Internet, and iPhones.

If you would have asked me, I suppose I would have told you there was a God, but I couldn't have given you a specific definition based on my experience. Perhaps that was because my Sunday school classes did much to help us memorize commandments but little to teach us who God was and how to relate to Him. Or perhaps they did, but I wasn't listening.

Nevertheless, my impersonal God served me fine. I had no need of the real thing. I didn't need a deity to reach down from heaven and wipe my nose, so none of it actually mattered. If God was on a dirt road walking toward me at that point, He was on the other side of a hill, and I hadn't begun to look for Him.

I started to sin about the time I turned 10. I sinned only in bits at first – small lies, little inconsistencies to teachers about homework. I learned the craft well – never looking my teacher in the eye, always speaking quickly from the diaphragm. Never feeble about the art of deception.

"Where is your homework?" my teacher would ask.

"I lost it."

"You lost it yesterday. You lost it last week."

"I am terrible about losing things. I need to learn." (Always be self-deprecating.)

"What am I going to do with you, Donald?"

"I am grateful for your patience." (Always be grateful.)

"I should call your mother."

"She's deaf. Boating accident. Piranha." (Always be dramatic. Use hand gestures.)

I also used a great deal of cusswords. Not those church cusswords – dang and darnit and so on. Big, robust cusswords, like the ones they use in PG movies. Cusswords are pure ecstasy when you are 12 or so, buzzing in the mouth like a battery on your tongue.

o o o

Across the street from my best friend Roy's house was a large, empty field divided by railroad tracks. It was there that I first identified with the biblical character Adam, because it was there that I saw my first naked woman.

We were playing with our bikes when Roy stumbled on a magazine. He approached the magazine with a stick, and I stood behind him as he flipped the pages from the distance of that twig. We had discovered a portal into a world of magic and wonder, where creatures exist in the purest form of beauty.

At last, Roy confronted the magazine by hand, slowly devouring its pages. He handed it to me after we dove deeper into the woods. We didn't speak – just turned the pages, addressing the miraculous forms whose beauty had not been matched by all the mountains and rivers. I felt like I had uncovered a secret – a secret that everybody in the world had known, but kept from me.

That night in my bed, my mind played the images, like scenes from a movie, delivering me into a sort of ecstasy from which I felt I'd never return. This new information seemed to give grass its green and sky its blue. Before I had even requested a reason to live, one had been delivered: naked women.

All of this gave way to my first encounter with guilt, which is still something inscrutable to me, as if aliens were sending transmissions from another planet, telling me there is a right and wrong in the universe. It wasn't only the sexual sins that brought guilt; it was lies and mean thoughts and throwing rocks at cars. My life had become something to hide. My thoughts were private. My lies were barriers that hid my thoughts. My tongue was a sharp weapon to protect the ugly me.

I would lock myself in a room, isolating myself from my sister and mother – not (usually) to sin, but simply because I had become a creature of odd secrecy. This is where my early ideas about religion came into play.

The ideas I had learned in Sunday school – about how we shouldn't sin – kept bugging me. I felt I needed to redeem myself, the way a kid feels when he finally decides to clean his room. My carnal thinking had made a mess of my head. I felt I was standing in the doorway of my mind, wondering where to begin – how to organize my thoughts so they weren't so out of control.

That's when I realized that religion might be able to get me back to normal, so I could have fun without feeling guilty. I didn't want to have to think about the guilt crap anymore.

For me, however, there was a mental wall between religion and God. I could walk around inside religion and never understand that God was a person, an actual being with thoughts and feelings. To me, God was more like a slot machine, doling out rewards based on behavior – or, perhaps, pure chance.

My slot-machine God provided relief from my guilt and gave me a sense of hope that my life would get organized. So, with more a sense of superstition than spirituality, I prayed for forgiveness, thinking the cherries might line up and the light atop the machine would flash, spilling shiny tokens of good fortune. And it worked. Something nice would happen to me, and I thought it was God.

"IF YOU COMPREHEND GOD HE IS NOT GOD."

— SAINT THOMAS AQUINAS

If something nice didn't happen, I went back to the slot machine, knelt in prayer, and pulled the lever a few more times. I liked this God very much, because you rarely had to talk to it, and it never talked back. But the fun didn't last.

My slot-machine God disintegrated on Christmas Eve when I was 13. The day remains one of the few times I can claim a direct encounter with God – one of those profound revelations that only God can induce.

That night I truly realized that other people had feelings and fears and that my interactions with them actually meant something. I could make them happy or sad, depending on how I associated with them. And not only could I make them happy or sad, I was responsible for the way I behaved. I was supposed to make them happy; I was not supposed to make them sad.

I know that that this sounds simple, but when you really get it for the first time, it hits you hard.

That Christmas, I bought my mom a shabby Christmas book whose contents would not interest her. I had money to buy presents, and I spent most of it to buy fishing equipment for myself.

My extended family opens gifts on Christmas Eve, while the immediate family opens gifts the next morning. So, in my room that night were wonderful presents – toys, games, candy. As I lay in bed, I counted and categorized them in the moonlight: the battery-operated toys of greatest importance, the underwear of no consequence at all.

As I drifted in and out of sleep, it hit me that I had bought my mother's gift with the petty change left after I had pleased myself. I put my mother's happiness behind my own material desires. The resulting guilt was different from anything I had felt before. It was heavy, and I couldn't do anything about it.

I fell out of bed, onto my knees, and begged God – not the slot-machine God, but a living, feeling God – to stop my pain. I crawled out of my room and into the hallway, by my mother's door. I lay there for an hour or so, sometimes succumbing to sleep, before the burden lifted and I was able to return to my room.

We opened the rest of our gifts on Christmas morning, and I was pleased to receive what I did. When my mother opened her silly book, I asked her forgiveness, telling her I wished I had done more. She pretended to enjoy the book, saying she wanted to know more about its subject.

I still felt terrible that evening when the family gathered for dinner, around a table so full of food that a kingdom could feast. I sat low in my chair, eye level with the bowls of potatoes and corn, having my hair straightened by ten talking women.

And while everyone ate and chatted away another Christmas, I felt ashamed, wondering silently if they knew they were eating with Hitler.

o o o

When I was young, I thought I had forever to figure things out – things like feeling like Hitler. But I didn't have that long. I believe the devil's greatest trick is not getting us into some kind of evil but in getting us to waste time. This is why the devil tries so hard to get Christians to be religious. If he can sink a man's mind into habit, that will prevent his heart from engaging God. I was into habit. I grew up going to church and became accustomed to hearing about God. He was like Uncle Harry or Aunt Sally, except we didn't have pictures of Him.

God never sent presents either. We had a dumpy house and a dumpy car, and I had zits. Looking back, I suppose God sent sunsets and forests and flowers, but what is that to a kid? The only thing I heard from God was what I heard on Christmas Eve, when He made me feel guilty. I didn't like that at all. I didn't feel like I knew God, yet He was making me experience conviction.

If you don't love someone, it gets annoying when he tells you what to do or what to feel. But when you love someone, you get pleasure from his pleasure, or her pleasure. It's easy to serve someone you love. But I didn't love God, because I didn't know God.

Still, I knew there was something wrong with me. And

not only with me — with everybody. It was like a bacteria or a cancer. It wasn't just on the skin; it was in the soul. It showed itself in loneliness, lust, anger, jealousy, and depression. It had people screwed up bad everywhere you went — at the store, at church, and at home. Singers on the radio were singing about it. Cops had jobs because of it.

o o o

I was watching *Nightline* a while ago, a feature on the Congo. Each of its eight tribes was at war with the other seven, the show informed me, and more than 2.5 million people had been killed in three years.

As the images moved across my TV screen, I felt so American and safe, as if the Congo were something in a book or a movie. It is nearly impossible for me to process the idea that a place like the Congo exists in the same world as Portland, Oregon.

I discussed the stuff on *Nightline* with Tony the Beat Poet. "I knew that was taking place," Tony said, "but I didn't know it was that bad." I call Tony a beat poet because he wears loose European shirts, the ones that lace up the chest with a shoestring. He shaves his head, and he has a long soul patch that stretches a good inch below his chin. He isn't actually a poet.

"It's terrible," I told him. "Two and a half million people dead. In one village, they interviewed about fifty women who had been raped. Most of them repeatedly."

Tony shook his head. "That is amazing. It is so difficult to process how things like that can happen."

"I know. I keep wondering how people could do things like that."

"Do you think you could do something like that, Don?"

"What are you talking about?"

Tony was looking at me seriously. "Are you capable of murder or rape or any of the stuff happening over there?"

"No. What are you getting at?"

"I just want to know what makes those guys over there any different from you and me. They are human. We are human. Why are we any better than them?"

Tony had me on this one. If I said I could commit atrocities like those in the Congo, that would make me evil. But if I said I couldn't, that would suggest I was better evolved than some of the men in the Congo – and I would have some explaining to do.

"You believe we *are* capable of those things, don't you,

Tony?"

He lit his pipe and breathed in until the tobacco glowed orange. "I think so, Don."

"What you are saying is that we have a sin nature, like the fundamentalist Christians say."

"Pretty much. It just explains a lot, you know."

"Actually," I said reluctantly, "I have always agreed with the idea that we have a sin nature. I don't think it looks exactly like the fundamentalists say it does, 'cause I know so many people who do great things. But I do buy the idea that we are flawed. Something in us is broken. I think it's easier to do bad things than good things. And there is something in this basic fact, some little clue to the meaning of the universe."

"Yeah," Tony said. "Some friends were over at my house, and they have a kid, about four or five years old, and they were telling me about child training. Later, I wondered why we have to train kids at all. I wondered, *If I had a couple of kids and trained one of them, taught him right from wrong – but didn't train the other kid at all – which would be the better kid.*"

"The kid you teach right from wrong, of course," I said.

"Of course. But that should tell us something about the human condition. We have to be *taught* to be good. That's the flaw in the human condition."

"Here's one," I said, agreeing with Tony. "Why do we need cops?"

"We would have chaos without cops," he said matter-of-factly. "Just look at the countries with corrupt police. It's anarchy."

"Anarchy," I repeated.

"Anarchy!" he confirmed.

"But sometimes I think that if there were no cops, I would be fine, and I probably would. I was taught right and wrong as a kid. But the truth is that I drive completely differently when there is a cop behind me, and when there isn't."

It is hard for us to admit we have a sin nature, because we live in this system of checks and balances. If we get caught, we'll be punished. But this doesn't make us good people; it makes us subdued people. Just think about the Senate and the House, even the President. The genius of the American system is checks and balances. Nobody gets all the powers. Everyone is watching everyone else. It's as if the founding fathers knew intrinsically that the soul of humanity, unwatched, is perverse.

o o o

I know someone who has twice cheated on his wife. He confessed this to me over coffee, after I told him how I thought humanity was, perhaps, broken – how, for us, doing good and moral things was like swimming upstream. He wondered if God had mysteriously told me about his infidelity. He squirmed a bit, then spoke to me as if I were a priest. He confessed everything.

I told him I was sorry, that it sounded terrible. It must have been terrible. His body was wracked with guilt and self-hatred. He said he would lie down next to his wife at night and feel a wall of concrete between their hearts. He has secrets. She tries to love him but knows he doesn't deserve it. He can't accept her affection because she is loving a man who doesn't exist. This guy was an actor in his own home.

Designed for good, my friend was sputtering and throwing smoke. The soul was not designed for this, I thought. We were supposed to be good, all of us. We were supposed to be good.

I believe that every well-adjusted human being has dealt squarely with his or her own depravity. I realize this sounds very Christian, very fundamentalist and browbeating, but I want to tell you that this part of what the Christians are saying is true. The path to joy winds through a dark valley. Jesus feels strongly about communicating the idea of our brokenness, so it is worthy of our reflection.

Nothing is going to change in the Congo until you and I figure out what is wrong with the person in the mirror.

o o o

As a teenager, there were certain aspects of Christian spirituality I liked, and aspects I thought were humdrum.

I associated much of Christian doctrine with children's stories because I grew up in a church. My Sunday school teachers had turned Bible narrative into children's fables. They talked about Noah and the ark and all of the animals. They failed to mention the part about God massacring most of humanity.

It confused me that some people would explore parts of the Bible, but not the whole thing. They ignored a lot of obvious questions. I thought Christianity was a product that kept falling apart, and whoever was selling it would hold the broken parts behind his back, trying to divert everyone's attention.

It took me a while to realize that stories like the Garden of Eden and Noah and the ark, while often told to children, weren't children's stories at all. I think the devil has tricked us into thinking that much of biblical theology is a story fit for kids.

How did we come to think that the story of Noah's ark is appropriate for children? Can you imagine a book about this event, complete with pictures of people gasping and flailing as they drown? Of mothers grasping for their children while they go flying down white-water rapids? Of children's tiny heads being bashed against rocks? A children's book like that wouldn't sell many copies.

So, I couldn't give myself to Christianity, because it was a religion for the intellectually naïve. To believe Christianity, you had to reduce enormous theological ideas into children's stories – or ignore the ideas altogether.

Help came from the most unlikely of sources. I took a college literature course in which we studied the elements of story: setting, conflict, climax, and resolution.

I started wondering why the heart and mind respond to this specific formula of stories. So I broke it down: Setting – that's easy. Every story has a setting. My setting is America, on earth. I understand setting because I experience setting.

Then there is conflict. Every good story has conflict. Some conflict is external, some internal, but if you want to write a novel that sells, you must have conflict. We understand conflict because we experience conflict, right? But where does conflict come from? Why do we have it in our lives?

Pondering these questions helped me a lot in accepting the idea of original sin and the birth of conflict. The rebellion against God explained why humans first experienced conflict in their lives. This felt like an epiphany: Without the Christian explanation of original sin – the seemingly silly story about Adam and Eve and the infamous tree – there was no explanation of conflict. None at all.

Now, some people view the Genesis account as a metaphor, not a literal event, but whether you take it literally or metaphorically, this event explains the human struggle that every person experiences: loneliness, crying yourself to sleep, addiction, pride, war, and self-obsession.

The heart responds to conflict in a story, I began to think, because there is some great conflict in the universe, and we are all experiencing it – even if only subconsciously.

If we weren't experiencing some conflict in our lives, our hearts would not respond to the conflict in books or film. The idea of having tension, suspense, or an enemy would make no sense to us. But they do.

Then there is the story element known as climax. Every good story has a climax – a point that determines how the story will end. As I thought about this, I got a bit scared. If the human heart uses the tools of reality to create elements of story, this means that a climax – or decision point – could very well be something that exists in the universe. Could there be a decision that the human heart needs to make? This was spooky to me because for thousands of years big-haired preachers have talked about the idea that we need to "make a decision" to follow or reject Christ. They would offer this idea as a sort of magical solution to the dilemma of life. I always hated hearing this, because it seemed an unfashionable thing to believe.

But maybe this unfashionable idea held something mystical and true. And perhaps I was judging the idea not on its merit, but on the style of those presenting it.

This climax element of story paralleled my understanding of Christian spirituality. Christianity offered a decision. It also offered a good and bad resolution. Our decisions were instrumental in the way our stories turned out.

o o o

A long time ago, I saw a folk singer in concert. Between songs, he told a story that helped me resolve some things about God. The story was about one of his friends, a Navy

SEAL. He told it like it was true, so I guess it is true.

The singer said his friend was performing a covert operation to free hostages from a building in some dark part of the world. The SEALs flew in by helicopter, made their way to the compound, and stormed the building where the hostages had been imprisoned for months. The building was filthy and dark, and the hostages were curled up in a corner, terrified.

When the SEALs entered, they heard the gasps of the hostages. They stood at the door and called out that they were Americans, asking the hostages to follow them. But the hostages wouldn't. They sat there on the floor and hid their eyes in fear. They didn't believe their rescuers were really Americans.

The SEALs stood there, not knowing what to do. Then the singer's friend had an idea. He put down his weapon, took off his helmet, and curled up next to the hostages. He put his arms around the hostages closest to him, trying to show that he was one of them. None of hostages' captors would have done something like this.

The SEAL sat with the hostages until some of them started to look at him, letting their eyes meet his. Then he whispered that he and his companions were Americans sent to rescue them. "Will you follow us?" he asked, rising to his feet. One of the hostages did the same, then another. Eventually, all were willing to go.

The story ends with all of the hostages safe on an American aircraft carrier.

I never liked how preachers said we had to follow Jesus. Sometimes they made Him sound angry or impatient. But I liked the folk singer's story. I liked the idea of Jesus becoming a man so that we would be able to trust

Him. And I liked that He healed people and loved them and cared deeply how they were feeling.

When I understood that the decision to follow Jesus was like the hostages' decision to follow their rescuer, I knew that I needed to decide if I would follow Jesus. The decision was simple once I asked myself, *Is Jesus the Son of God, are we being held captive in a world run by Satan – a world filled with brokenness – and do I believe Jesus can rescue me?*

As I answered those questions, I realized that if life had a climax, which it must for the element of climax to be mirrored in life's story, then Christian spirituality offered a climax. It offered a decision.

The last element of story is resolution. Christian spirituality also offered me a resolution, the resolution of forgiveness and a home in the afterlife. Again, this all sounded witless to me at first. But then I reached a point in my life where I desperately wanted to believe it. I felt like my soul was designed to live the story that Christian spirituality was telling. I felt like my soul yearned to be forgiven. I wanted the resolution God was offering me.

So there it was: setting, conflict, climax, and resolution. As silly as it seemed at one point, Christian spirituality met the requirements of the heart – and it matched the facts of reality. It felt more than true; it felt meaningful. I started to believe that I was a character in a greater story, which is why the elements of story made sense in the first place.

The proposition of the gospel, once free from the clasps of fairy tale, became very adult to me, very gritty, like something from Hemingway or Steinbeck – with copious amounts of sex and blood. Christian spirituality was not a children's story. It wasn't cute or neat. It was mystical and odd and clean – yet it was reaching into dirty. There was wonder in it.

2

OF

FAITH
AND GRACE

Portland, where I live, is home to Reed College. Some of Portland's Christians talk about Reed as if it's Hades. They say Reed's students are pagans, heathens. Reed was recently selected by the *Princeton Review* as the college where students are most likely to ignore God.

There are no rules at Reed, and many of the students have issues with authority. But they are also brilliant. Loren Pope, former education editor at *The New York Times*, calls Reed "the most intellectual college in the country." Per capita, Reed receives more awards and fellowships than any other U.S. college. It has produced more than 30 Rhodes scholars.

My friend Ross had a son, Michael, who attended Reed. When Ross and I would get together to talk, he would tell me that Michael was not doing well. He had impregnated his girlfriend, and after the birth the girl didn't allow Michael to see the child. During Michael's senior year at Reed, he committed suicide, jumping off a cliff on the Oregon coast.

I never knew Michael, but everybody who did loved him. After he died, Reed students flooded his in-box with goodbye letters and notes of grief and disbelief. In the years after Michael's death, Reed remained in the back of my mind.

Eventually, I started thinking of going back to school. I wasn't sure what to study, and I have always been a terrible student. Deadlines and tests do me in. I can't take the pressure. But Tony the Beat Poet told me he was considering auditing an Ancient Greek Literature class; he asked me to join him.

At the time, I was attending a large church in the suburbs. It was like worshiping at The Gap. I don't know why I attended. I didn't fit in. When I told some church people I wanted to audit classes at Reed, they looked at me as if I wanted to date Satan. One friend even told me that God did not want me to attend Reed.

o o o

My first day at Reed was exhilarating. Reed had ashtrays, and everybody cussed. There were 400 freshmen in my Greek Lit class, and I understood about 10 percent of my first lecture. But that 10 percent was brilliant. I loved it.

After class, I would usually go to the Commons to get coffee and organize my notes. It was at the Commons that I met Laura, an atheist who would teach me a lot about God. Her father was a Methodist minister. She was the only one in her family who couldn't embrace the idea of

God. She explained to me that her family loved her all the same, and that there was no tension because of her resistance to faith.

Laura and I met every day after lectures to rehash the day's themes. I've never met anybody as brilliant as Laura. She seemed to understand the complicated themes like they were children's cartoons.

"What did you think of the lecture?" I once asked her.

"I thought it was okay. This is supposed to be a pretty challenging school, and I wasn't that challenged. I hope they don't put the cookies on a lower shelf all year."

"Cookies?" I asked. (I thought she had cookies.)

Then Laura went on to explain ideas I didn't understand. In time, she learned I was a Christian, but we didn't talk much about it.

At one point, though, she asked me about racism in

America and whether the church had been a harbor for that sort of hatred. I answered that, for the most part, I thought evangelical churches failed pretty badly during the civil rights movement, as did most other social institutions.

I went on to tell her how frustrating it is to be a Christian in America, and how frustrated I was with the church's human-rights failures – and my own personal failure to contribute to the solution. I wondered aloud, though, if there was a bigger issue than racism. I suggested that racism might be a minor problem compared to bigger trouble we have to deal with.

"Racism, not an issue?!" Laura questioned sternly. "How can you say that? Don, it's an enormous problem."

"Yeah, I understand it is a terrible and painful problem, but in light of the whole picture, racism is a signal of something greater. There is a larger problem here than tension between ethnic groups."

"Unpack that statement."

"I'm talking about self-absorption. The human race is self-absorbed. As a human, I am flawed in that it is difficult for me to consider others before myself. It feels like I have to fight against this force within me that wants to avoid serious issues and please myself. Buy things for myself. Feed myself. Entertain myself. All I am saying is that if we, as humans, could fix our self-absorption, we could end a lot of pain in the world."

Laura didn't say much more that afternoon, but several weeks later, she hinted that she agreed with me about the problem of self-absorption. But she called the problem sin.

"Wait," I said, "How can you believe in sin but not in God?"

"I just do."

"But you can't."

"I can do what I want."

"Okay," I said, knowing that if I argued with her, she would win.

Laura and I didn't talk much about religion after that. She dreamed of becoming a writer, so we talked about literature. She would give me articles or essays she had written. I ate them up. They were terrific. It was an honor just to know her. And I could sense deeply that God wanted a relationship with Laura. Ultimately, I believe God loves and wants a relationship with every human being, but with Laura I could feel God's urgency. Laura, however, never brought up the idea of God, so I didn't either.

◦   ◦   ◦

Only a few students at Reed claimed to be Christians, and though I was only auditing classes, they accepted me into their group. We met in the chapel to pray each week, and we held Bible studies in one of the dorm rooms. It was very underground.

Reed has traditionally resisted Christianity. The previous year, for Easter Sunday, a few Christians had created a small meditation room on campus. They dimmed the lights in a room in the library, lit some candles, and let students know the room was available if anybody wanted to pray or meditate.

When Easter morning rolled around, some students decided to protest. They bought a keg of beer, got drunk, and "slaughtered" a stuffed lamb in the room.

The Christians at Reed were Christlike about it. I learned so much from them. I learned that true love turns the other cheek, doesn't take a wrong into account, and loves all people, regardless of their indifference or hostility. These people seemed to me, well, revolutionary. I knew that Laura would fit in with them. And I sensed that no matter how far she was from God, she could come to know Him.

o   o   o

The goofy thing about Christian faith is that you believe it and don't believe it at the same time. It's like having an imaginary friend. I believe in Jesus, believe He's the Son of God. But every time I try to explain this to somebody, I feel like a palm reader, or like a Trekkie at a Star Trek convention, who hasn't figured out that the show isn't real.

Until.

When one of my friends becomes a Christian – which happens about every 10 years because I am such a sheep about sharing my faith – the experience is euphoric. I see in the friend's eyes the trueness of the story.

At one point, everybody at Reed was telling me there was something wrong with Laura. They said she was depressed or something. I ran into her at a lecture. She sat in front of me, and when the lecture ended she didn't leave. Neither did I. I didn't want to bother her, but I could tell she was about to say something.

"How are you?" I asked.

"I am not good." She turned to face me. I could tell she had spent the morning crying.

"What's wrong?"

"Everything."

I asked it was boy stuff or school stuff. She said no. Then I asked, "God stuff?"

Her eyes were moist. "I guess so, Don."

"Can you explain any of it? The way you feel."

"I feel like my life is a mess."

"I see."

"I just want to confess. I have done terrible things. Can I confess to you?"

"I don't think confessing to me is going to do you any good."

Laura wiped her eyes with her fingers. "I feel like He's after me, Don."

"Who is after you?"

"God."

"I think that is very beautiful, Laura. And I believe you. I believe God wants you. What do you think He wants?"

"FAITH IS THE COURAGE TO ACCEPT ACCEPTANCE."

— PAUL TILLICH

"I don't know. But you don't understand. I can't do this."

"Can't do what?"

"Be a Christian."

"Why can't you be a Christian?"

Laura didn't answer. She just looked at me and rolled her tired eyes. She dropped her hands into her lap with a sigh. "I wish I could read you my journal," she said. "Part of me wants to believe. I wrote about it. My family believes, Don. I feel as though I need to believe. Like I am going to die if I don't believe. But it is all so stupid."

"Laura, why is it that you hang out with Christians on campus?"

"I don't know. I guess I am just curious. I don't think you're dumb. I just don't understand how you can believe this stuff."

I told her that I really didn't know how either. But I said

I did believe in God – that something inside me caused me to believe. And that He wanted Laura to believe too.

"I think God wants a relationship with you," I explained, "and that starts with confessing directly to Him. He is offering forgiveness."

"You're not making this easy," she said. "I don't exactly believe I need a God to forgive me of anything."

"I know. But that is what I believe is happening. Perhaps you can see it as an act of social justice. The entire world is falling apart because nobody will admit being wrong. But by asking God to forgive you, you are willing to own your own crap."

"I can't get there. I can't just say it without meaning it. It would be like trying to fall in love with somebody. You don't decide that. It just happens. If God is real, He needs to happen to me."

"That is true. But don't panic. God brought you this far; He will bring you the rest of the way. It may take time."

"But this hurts. I want to believe, but I can't. I hate this!"

Then Laura went back to her room.

o   o   o

I had no explanation for Laura. I don't think there is an explanation. My belief in Jesus didn't seem rational or scientific, and I think Laura was looking for something rational. She believed that all things that were true were also rational. But that isn't the case. Love is a true emotion, but it's not rational. It's something you feel.

I have been in love. Plenty of people have been in love. Yet love can't be proven scientifically. Neither can beauty. Even light cannot be proved scientifically, yet we all believe in light and use light to see things. There are plenty of true things that don't make any sense. One of Laura's problems was that she wanted God to make sense. He doesn't. He will make no more sense to me than I will make sense to an ant.

One day I talked to Tony the Beat Poet about Laura, and we started discussing belief – what it takes to believe. He asked me how I believed in God.

I felt silly trying to explain it, even though Tony is a Christian. I felt as if I were saying I believed in Peter Pan or the Tooth Fairy, and I don't believe in Peter Pan or the Tooth Fairy. I believe in God, and, as I've said before, it feels so much more like something is causing me to believe than I am stirring up belief inside myself. In fact, I go as far as to say that when I started in faith I didn't want to believe. My intellect wanted to disbelieve, but my soul, the deeper instinct, could no more stop believing in God than

Tony could, on a whim, stop being in love with his wife.

There are things you choose to believe, and beliefs that choose you. Christian faith was one that chose me.

In his book *Orthodoxy*, G.K. Chesterton says chess players go crazy, not poets. I think he's right. You'd go crazy trying to explain certain things. I don't think you can explain how Christian faith works. It is a mystery. And I love this about Christian spirituality. It cannot be explained, yet it is beautiful and true. It is something you feel, and it comes from the soul.

o o o

A few days after my conversation with Tony, I crawled out of bed and cracked open the Bible on my desk. I didn't feel like reading, so I turned on my computer and fidgeted with a SimCity town I had been working on. Then I checked my emails and noticed one from Laura. She had sent it in the early hours of that morning. The subject line read: So, anyway, about all of that stuff . . .

Dearest Friend Don,

I read through the book of Matthew this evening. I was up all night. I couldn't stop reading, so I read through Mark. This Jesus of yours is either a madman or the Son of God. Somewhere in the middle of Mark, I realized He was the Son of God. I suppose this makes me a Christian. I feel much better now. Come to campus tonight and let's get coffee.

Much love,
Laura

o o o

My pastor, Rick, is one of my best friends. He became a Christian when he was 19. Before he became a Christian, he played football for Chico State, which at the time was the No. 1 party school in the nation. Rick did his share of partying. After months of drunken binges, though, he began to wonder if there was more to life than alcohol and sex. He began to long for God. So the next Sunday morning, he made a point of being sober and walked to a local church.

This was Rick's first time stepping inside a church, and the pastor happened to talk about sin, and how we are all sinners. He also talked about Jesus, and how Jesus died so that God could forgive us of our sin. At the end of the service, Rick prayed and became a Christian.

A few weeks later, the pastors from Rick's new church visited him, each in his suit and tie. Rick entertained them and made them coffee, all of them sipping coffee and chatting – while the smell of marijuana drifted in from an adjoining room, where Rick's friend was smoking pot. Rick laughs when he tells me he offered the pastors a hit. He says he wasn't too offended when they turned him down.

The pastors talked to Rick about his conversion, explaining that he had been forgiven of his sins and that it was important to try to live a righteous life. Rick agreed with them, noting how much easier it would be to listen to a Sunday-morning sermon if he didn't have a hangover.

Rick began to choose purity over sin. He did well for a while. But soon he found himself wanting to party with his friends or have sex with his girlfriend, and he occasionally failed in his efforts to be moral. Rick tells me that those were the most depressing moments of his life, because he felt he was failing the God who saved him.

Rick was anguished by his inability to control his desires. He felt he had been given a new life – and the key to heaven – yet he couldn't obey Jesus in return. One evening, he got on his knees and told God he was sorry. He told God how much he wished he could be good and obedient. Then he swallowed enough muscle relaxants and sleeping kills to kill three people. He lay down in a fetal position and waited to die.

o o o

Looking back on that night, Rick tells me that he was too proud to receive free grace from God. He didn't know how to live in a system in which nobody owes anybody else anything. And the harder it was for Rick to repay God, the more he wanted to hide from God. His life was torture.

For a long time, I couldn't understand why some people had no trouble accepting God's grace, while others experience great difficulty. I counted myself as one of those who had trouble. I would hear about grace, read about grace, and even sing about grace. But accepting grace was an action I could not understand. It seemed wrong to avoid paying for my sins – to not feel guilty and kick myself around. More than that, grace wasn't something I was truly looking for. It was too easy. I wanted to feel like I *earned* my forgiveness, as though God and I were buddies doing favors for each other.

Enlightenment came in an unexpected place: a grocery store. At a Safeway checkout counter, the lady in front of me pulled out food stamps to pay for her groceries. I had never seen food stamps before. They were more colorful than I imagined and looked more like money than stamps. As she unfolded her currency, I could tell that she, the checkout girl, and I were all uncomfortable. I wished there was something I could do, maybe pay for the groceries myself.

The checkout girl quickly performed her job, signing and verifying a few documents, then ushered the lady through the line. That woman never lifted her head as she organized her bags of groceries and put them in her cart. Then she walked away stiffly, like a person does when she knows she's being watched.

As I drove away, I realized that I, not that woman, should be pitied. Somehow I had come to believe that just because a person is needy she is a candidate for sympathy, not just charity. It wasn't really that I wanted to buy her groceries;

the government was already doing that. I wanted to buy her dignity. But by judging her, I took her dignity away.

I wonder what it would be like – using food stamps for a month. I wonder how that would feel, standing in line, pulling from my wallet the bright currency of poverty, feeling customers' probing eyes as they studied the items in my cart. I would want to explain to them that I had a job and made money. Maybe just not enough.

I love to give to charity, but I don't want to be charity. This is why I have so much trouble with grace.

A few years ago, I was listing prayer requests to a friend. I mentioned my friends and family, but not my personal problems. My friend candidly asked me to reveal my own struggles, but I told him they weren't that bad. He answered in the confident voice of a teacher, "Don, you are not above the charity of God."

In that instant, he revealed that my motives weren't noble, but prideful. I didn't care more about my friends than myself; I believed I was above God's grace. Like Rick, I was too prideful to accept grace.

I want to earn my own way so that I won't be a charity case.

○   ○   ○

Rick tells me that as he lay there waiting to die, he heard God say, "Your life is not your own, but you have been bought with a price." With these words, Rick felt peace. He understood cognitively and emotionally that his role in his relationship with God was to humbly receive God's unconditional love.

Rick, of course, is still alive – a miracle he cannot

explain. The pills put him to sleep before he could make any effort to save himself, but he woke the next morning with ample energy, as if he had never swallowed the pills.

After surviving the suicide attempt, Rick went to Bible college, married a girl he met there, and now they have four children. A while ago, he planted a church in downtown Portland, widely considered the most unchurched region in the country. Only about eight of us attended the first meeting. Today that church has grown to more than 500 people. On any given Sunday dozens of nonbelievers attend our church, and Rick always shares with them the patient love of God. He talks about Jesus as if he really knows Him, as if they've talked on the phone earlier that day. Rick loves God because he accepts God's unconditional love first.

Rick says I will love God because He first loved me. I will obey God because I love God. But if I cannot accept

God's love, I cannot love Him in return – and I won't be able to obey Him. Self-discipline will never make us feel righteous or clean; accepting God's love will. Accepting God's grace and ferocious love is the fuel we need.

The devil doesn't want us to accept God's love and kindness. He's the voice in our head, saying we are losers and failures, that we'll never amount to anything. Satan is the voice trying to convince the bride that her groom doesn't really love her. This is not God's voice. God woos us with kindness. He changes our character with the passion of His love.

Self-discipline alone won't change behavior for long. But fall in love, and a human will accomplish things he never dreamed possible. The laziest man will swim the English Channel to win his woman. What Rick said is worth repeating: By accepting God's love for us, we fall in love with Him, and only then do we have the fuel to obey.

In exchange for our humility and willingness to accept God's charity, we are given a kingdom. And a beggar's kingdom is better than a proud man's delusion.

TRUE
CONFESSIONS 3

When I moved to downtown Portland to attend Imago Dei, the church Rick started, I learned how serious he was about loving people regardless of whether or not they considered Jesus the Son of God. Rick wanted to love them because they were hungry, thirsty, or lonely. The human struggle bothered Rick, as if something was broken in the world, and we were supposed to hold our palms against the wound.

Rick didn't see evangelism – or whatever you want to call it – as a target on a wall. He saw it as reaching a felt need. I thought this was beautiful and frightening. Beautiful, because I had the same need; I need Jesus like I need water or food. Frightening, because Christianity seems so stupid to so much of our culture, and I absolutely hate bothering people with this stuff.

In large part, I believe strongly in letting people live their own lives, and when I share my faith I feel like a network marketing guy trying to build my down-line. Some of my non-Christian friends think that Christians are insistent, demanding, and intrusive, but that isn't the case. Those kinds of Christians are the squeaky wheel. Most of us have enormous respect for others' space and freedom. It's just that we have found a joy in Jesus that we want to share.

For me, the beginning of sharing my faith with people came when I threw out religion and embraced true Christian spirituality — a mysterious, non-political system that can be experienced, but not explained. The term "Christianity" didn't excite me the way *Christian spirituality* did. And I could not, in good conscience, tell a friend about something that didn't excite me. I couldn't share something I wasn't experiencing myself. And, at this time in my life, I wasn't experiencing Christianity; it didn't do anything for me at all. It felt like math – a system of rights and wrongs. It wasn't mysterious – God reaching out of heaven to do wonderful things in my life. I loved talking about Jesus and the spirituality that comes from a relationship with Him, but sharing Christianity with someone would have felt like convincing someone to agree with me, not to meet God.

Tony the Beat Poet says the church is like a wounded animal these days. We used to have power and influence, but now we don't, and so many church leaders are upset about this, acting like spoiled children who are mad because they can't have their own way. They want to take their ball and go home because they have to sit on the bench.

Tony and I agree that God wants us to sit on the bench, in humility, and turn the other cheek. Like Gandhi, like Jesus. We decided that the right place to share our faith from was a place of love and humility, not power.

Each year, Reed hosts a festival called Ren Fayre. They shut down the campus so the students can party. Campus security keeps the authorities away, and everybody gets drunk and high, and some people get naked. The school even brings in a medical unit that specializes in treating bad drug trips.

Some of the Christians in our little group at Reed decided this event marked a good time to come out of the closet and let everybody know there were a few Christians on campus. We wondered what to do, because in the past, some students had expressed hostility toward Christians. I suggested we build a confession booth in the middle of campus, with a sign that said "Confess your sins." I meant it as a joke, but Tony thought it was brilliant.

"But here's the catch," he told our little group, "We are not actually going to accept confessions. We are going to confess that, as followers of Jesus, we have not been very loving. We have been bitter, and for that we are sorry. We will apologize for the Crusades, we will apologize for the televangelists, and we will apologize for neglecting the poor and lonely. We will ask the students to forgive us, and we will tell them that in our selfishness we have misrepresented Jesus. We will tell people who come to our booth that Jesus loves them."

We all sat there in silence because it was obvious that something beautiful and true had hit with a thud. We all thought it was a great idea.

For so much of my life, I had been defending Christianity, because I thought to admit that we had done any wrong would discredit our whole religious system. But I realized that it isn't about a religious system; it's about people following Christ. The important thing to do, the right thing to do, was to apologize for getting in the way of Jesus.

I prayed about getting in the confession booth. I wondered if I could apologize and mean it. I wondered if I could humble myself to a culture that, to some degree, had wronged Christians. But I looked in the eyes of my friends Penny and Iven, and I could see that this is what they wanted; they wanted to reach out to these people, their friends, and it didn't matter what it cost. They didn't care how much they had been hurt, and they certainly had more scars than Tony or I.

So we bought some wood and stored it in my garage. We went to the Thesis parade on Friday night and watched everyone get drunk and beat drums and dance in the spray of beer. Tony and I dressed like monks and smoked pipes and walked amid the anarchy. People approached us and asked what we were doing. We said that the next day we would be on campus to take confessions. They looked at us in amazement, asking if we were serious. We told them to come see us.

The next morning, while everyone was sleeping off a hangover, we started building the booth. It ended up being much larger than I expected, with two sections inside, one for the monk and one for the confessor. We put up a curtain as an entryway, and our friend Nadine painted "Confession Booth" in large letters on the outside of the booth.

o   o   o

Saturday night at Ren Fayre is alive and fun. The sun goes down, and they shoot fireworks. Students lie out on a hill and point at the sky in bleary-eyed fascination. The highlight of the evening is a "glow opera" designed to enhance mushroom trips. The actors wear black and carry colorful puppets and cutouts that come alive in the black light. Everybody oohs and ahhs.

Late in the evening, we lit tiki torches and mounted them outside our booth. I got in the booth and sat on a bucket. I could hear a rave happening in the student center. Nobody is going to confess, I thought. Who wants to stop dancing and go confess sins? I began to worry that this wasn't God's idea. Nobody was going to get angry at us, I thought, but nobody was going to care either.

I sat there wondering if Christian spirituality was true. You never question the truth of anything until you have to explain it to a skeptic, and I didn't feel like explaining. I didn't like being in the booth wearing a stupid monk outfit. I wanted to go to the rave. Everybody there was cool; we were just religious.

I was going to tell Tony I wanted to leave when he said

we had our first customer.

"What's up, man?" the student said with a smile. He told me my pipe smelled good.

I asked his name. He told me it was Jake, and I shook his hand, because I didn't know what else to do.

"So," he said, "what is this? Am I supposed to tell you all of the juicy gossip I did at Ren Fayre?"

"No, that's really not what we're doing."

"What's the deal, man. What's with the monk outfit?"

"Well, we are a group of Christians on campus, and we were thinking about the way Christians have sort of wronged people over time. You know, the Crusades, all that stuff...."

"Well, I doubt you were personally involved in any of that, man."

"No, I wasn't. But the thing is, we are followers of Jesus. We believe that He is God and all, and He repre-

"IT IS NO USE WALKING ANYWHERE TO PREACH, UNLESS OUR WALKING IS OUR PREACHING."

— ST. FRANCIS

sented certain ideas that we have not done a good job of representing."

"I see."

"So this group of us on campus wants to confess to you."

"You are confessing to me!" Jake said with a laugh.

"Yeah."

"You're serious."

I told him I was. He looked at me and told me I didn't have to confess. I told him I did.

"What are you confessing?" he asked.

I shook my head and looked at the ground. "Everything. Jesus said to feed the poor and heal the sick. I have never done very much about that. Jesus said to love those who persecute me. I tend to lash out. Jesus did not mix His spirituality with politics. I grew up doing that. I know a lot of people will not listen to the words of Christ because of people like me, who know Him but carry our own agendas into conversation rather than just relaying the message Jesus wants to get across. There's a lot more, you know."

"It's all right, man," Jake said, very tenderly. His eyes were starting to water.

"Well," I said, clearing my throat, "I'm sorry for all of that."

"I forgive you," Jake said. And he meant it.

He sat there awhile. "It's really cool what you guys are doing," he said. "A lot of people need to hear this."

"Have we hurt a lot of people?"

"You haven't hurt me. I just think it isn't popular to be a Christian, especially at a place like this. I don't think too many people have been hurt. Most of us just have a strong reaction to what we see on television. All these well-dressed preachers supporting the Republicans."

"That's not the whole picture. That's just television. I have friends who are giving their lives to feed the poor and defend the defenseless. They are doing it for Christ."

"You really believe in Jesus, don't you?"

"Yes. Most often I do. I have doubts at times, but mostly I believe in Him. It's like there is something in me that causes me to believe, and I can't explain it."

"You said earlier that there was a central message of Christ. I don't really want to become a Christian, but what is that message?"

"The message is that humanity sinned against God, and God gave the world over to humanity. If people want to be rescued, Christ will rescue them if they want. If they ask forgiveness for being part of the rebellion against God, then God will forgive them."

"What's the deal with the cross?"

"God says the wages of sin is death. Jesus died so that none of us would have to. If we have faith in that, then we are Christians."

"That is why people wear crosses?"

"I guess. I think it is sort of fashionable. Some people believe that if they have a cross around their neck, it has some sort of mystical power."

"Do you believe that?"

"No," I told Jake. I said that I thought mystical power came through faith in Jesus.

Then he asked me what I believed about God.

"I don't know," I answered. "I guess I didn't believe for a long time. The science of it is sort of sketchy. I guess I believe in God though. I believe somebody is responsible for all of this, this world we live in. And, Jake, if you want to know God, you can. I am just saying that if you ever want to call on Jesus, He will be there."

"Thanks, man. I believe you mean that." His eyes were watering again. "This is cool what you guys are doing. I am going to tell my friends about this."

"I don't know whether to thank you or not," I laughed. "I have to sit here and confess all my crap."

He looked at me seriously. "It's worth it," he said. He shook my hand, and when he left the booth there was somebody else waiting. It went on like that for a couple of hours. I talked to about 30 people, and Tony "took confessions" at a picnic table outside the booth. A lot of people wanted to hug us when we were done.

All of the people who visited us were grateful and gracious. I was being changed through the process. I went in with doubts and came out believing so strongly in Jesus that I was ready to die and be with Him. I think that night was the beginning of change for a lot of us.

After the event, Iven started taking a group of students to a local homeless shelter to feed the poor, and he often had to turn people away, because the van wouldn't hold more than 20 or so.

And we held an event called Poverty Day, when we asked students to live on less than three dollars a day, to practice solidarity with the poor. More than 100 students participated.

Penny spoke in Vollum Lounge on the topic of poverty in India; more than 75 students attended. Before any of this, our biggest event drew about ten people.

We hosted an evening and asked students to voice their hostility against Christians. We answered questions about what we believed and explained our love for people, for the hurting. We apologized again for our own wrongs against humanity and asked for forgiveness from the Reed community. We enjoyed the new friendships we made, and at one point we had four separate Bible studies on campus, specifically for people who didn't consider themselves Christians. We saw a lot of students take a second look at Christ. But mostly, we just felt right with the people around us. We felt forgiven and grateful.

On the night we took confessions, at about three in the morning, I was walking off campus with my monk robe under my arm. When I reached the large oak trees on the edge of the front lawn, I turned and looked at the campus. It looked so smart and old, and I could see lights coming from the Student Center. I could hear music thumping. Some kids were making out on the lawn and chasing each other down the sidewalks. There was laughing and dancing and vomiting.

I felt strongly that Jesus was relevant at Reed. I felt strongly that if He weren't relevant here, He was not relevant anywhere. I felt peaceful, sober. I felt very connected to God because I had confessed so much to so many people and had gotten so much off my chest. I had been forgiven by the people I had wronged with my indifference and judgmentalism. I decided to sit awhile, but it was cold and the grass was damp. So I went home and fell asleep on the couch.

The next morning I made coffee and sat on the porch at Graceland and wondered whether the things that happened the night before were real. I was out of the closet now. A Christian. So many years before, I had made amends to God, but now I had made amends to the world. I was someone willing to share my faith. I felt kind of cool, kind of different. It was very relieving.

ON
WORSHIP
AND WONDER

4

Someone asked Mother Teresa where she found the strength to love so many people, especially people ravaged by poverty and disease. She answered that she loved people because they are Jesus, each one of them. This is what the Bible teaches.

Mother Teresa's answer was poetic, but also illogical. Everyone can't be Jesus. That contradicts the facts of reality, as we see them. Some Christians struggle with aspects of their faith when they don't line up with logic. "If it's not logical," they contend, "it can't be true."

But the world abounds with things our hearts believe, even though they make no sense in our heads . . .

Beauty

Love

Jesus as God

It comforts me to think that if we are created beings, the thing that created us would have to be much greater than we are, greater than our understanding. If we could understand everything about God, would we be in awe of him? Would we consider him worthy of our worship?

When we worship God, we show our adoration and praise to a Being our minds and life experiences don't give us all the tools to understand. For example, God is eternal. Eternity is something the human mind can't grasp. Have you ever tried to contemplate how a Being could have no beginning and no end? Can we understand what it means to have never been born?

And yet, we believe that God is eternal. Christians, like everybody else, believe things we cannot explain.

A friend of mine, a seminary student, criticizes

some Christian writers for embracing what he calls "mysticism."

"So," I asked him, "does that mean that you're not a mystic?"

"Of course not," he said.

"Do you believe in the Trinity?"

"Yes."

Then I asked him if he believed that the Trinity represented three separate persons who are also one. He said he did.

Then I asked him, "Wouldn't that be considered a mystical idea?"

He just stood there, thinking.

You cannot be a Christian, can't truly worship God, without being a mystic.

o   o   o

At a Laundromat, I was talking with a homeless man, and he said that when we reduce Christian spirituality to math, we defile the Holy. I found this beautiful, and comforting, because I have never been good at math.

Many of our attempts to understand and define Christian faith have only cheapened it. I can no more understand the totality of God than the pancake I made for breakfast understands my complexity.

The good news is, though, that the little bit we do understand – that grain of sand our minds *are* capable of grasping – is enough to keep our hearts celebrating God's majesty forever. We don't know it all, but we know that God is good, that God feels, that God knows all, that God loves us.

○ ○ ○

One summer, I made a point to catch sunsets. I would ride my motorcycle up Mount Tabor and sit on the steps of a reservoir to watch the sun put fire in the clouds that always hang over Portland. I never really wanted to make the trip; I would have preferred to watch television or make a sandwich. But I made myself go. And once I got there, I always loved it. It meant something to me – seeing the beauty over my city.

From the ridge on Tabor, I could see the entire skyline, the home of more than a million people. On most nights, no more than two or three people were with me. Think about it: All that beauty happens right above the heads of more than a million humans who never notice it.

"WHEN WE REDUCE CHRISTIAN SPIRITUALITY TO MATH, WE DEFILE THE HOLY."

– HOMELESS MAN
IN A PORTLAND LAUNDROMAT

All of the wonder of God happens right above our arithmetic and formulas. I have found that the more I climb outside my pat answers, the more invigorating the view. And the more my heart enters into worship.

o   o   o

I love how the Gospels begin – with John the Baptist eating bugs and baptizing people. Some religious leaders sought baptism because it had become popular. John yelled at them, calling them snakes, and telling them that the baptismal waters wouldn't do anything for them but get their snakeskins wet.

He said that only if they believed in the sacrament of baptism – if they had faith that Jesus was real and that he was coming to transform the world – then Jesus would ignite the Kingdom life within them. I love this, because for so long my religion had no magic in it. No wonder in it. No fire burned in my chest.

So, now when I get tempted to lapse into that lifeless brand of religion, I go back to the Gospels for the comfort of knowing that there is a faith that rises above the emptiness of ritual. God will ignite the Kingdom life within us, the Bible promises. That's mysticism. It's not a formula we can figure out. It's just something God does for us.

o o o

My friend Jason and I went on a trip to Joshua Tree and Death Valley, and he had a map folded across his lap for nearly the whole trip. Even when I was driving, he sat with the map, his finger tracing the trajectory of the car, noting how close we were to certain towns, certain lakes. Jason liked to know where we were on the map, and so did I. But I was afraid to tell him about the universe, how scientists haven't found the edge of it – how nobody knows exactly where we are on the map.

We have two choices in the face of such big beauty: terror or awe. And this is precisely why we try to chart God. We want to be able to predict Him, to dissect Him, to carry Him around for our little dog-and-pony show. We are too proud to feel awe, too fearful to feel terror. So we reduce God to math. That way, we don't have to fear Him. But the Bible tells us that fear is the appropriate response, that fear of God is the beginning of wisdom. Does this mean that God is going to hurt us? No. But I stood on the edge of the Grand Canyon once, behind a railing, and though I was safe from tumbling over the edge, I feared the mere thought of it. It is that big of a place, that wonderful of a landscape.

o   o   o

In the movie *Dead Poets Society*, I like the scene in which English teacher Mr. Keating, played by Robin Williams, instructs his students to rip out the "Introduction to Poetry" essay in their literature textbooks. The essay outlines a formula for "grading" poetry, complete with a sliding numeric scale and grid, thus reducing art for the heart to math for the head. Keating dismisses the formula as rubbish.

At first, the students look around at each other in confusion. Then, at their teacher's vigorous prodding, they begin to rip at the pages. Keating paces the aisles with a trash can, reminding his students that poetry is not algebra, not songs on *American Bandstand*, which can be rated on a scale of 1 to 100. Poems, he explains, are pieces of art that plunge into the depths of the heart, to stir vigor in men and woo women.

Too much of our time is spent charting God on a grid. Too little time is spent allowing our hearts to feel awe. So, by reducing Christian spirituality to formula, we deprive our hearts of wonder.

When I think about the complexity of the Trinity, the three-in-one God, my mind can't understand it. But my heart feels wonder, abundantly satisfying wonder. It's like my heart is saying to my mind, *You cannot understand some things, and you must learn to live with this. Not only must you learn to live with this, you must learn to* enjoy *this.*

Here's something about me that you might see as a weakness. (You might feel that you have this "weakness" too.) I need wonder. I know that death is coming. I smell it in the wind, read it in the paper, watch it on TV, and see it on the faces of the old. So I need wonder to explain what is going to happen to me, what is going to happen to *us,* when this life is done. When our shift is over and our kids' kids are still on the earth, listening to their crazy rap music. I need something mysterious to happen after I die. I need to be somewhere else after I die. Somewhere with God. Somewhere that wouldn't make sense if it were explained to me right now.

At the end of the day, when I lie in bed and know that the chances of any of our various theologies being exactly right are about a million to one, I take comfort that God has things figured out. So even if my math is wrong, we are still going to be okay. Wonder is the feeling we get when we do just that – let go of our silly answers, our mapped-out rules that we want God to follow. And I don't believe that there is any better worship than wonder.

ALL
ABOUT
LOVE

5

For a while, my friend Paul and I lived in the woods, with hippies. Well, sort of hippies. (They certainly smoked a lot of pot and drank a lot of beer.) And man did they love each other. Sometimes too much, sometimes too physically. But they loved. They accepted and even cherished everybody, even the ones who judged them because they were hippies.

These weren't nomadic, live-off-the-land (and off of other people) hippies. They were formally educated – studying at NYU, getting master's degrees in literature, or heading off to law school. That sort of thing. They knew all about Hopkins, Poe, and Plath. They knew the Americans and the Brits and the fashionable African, Cuban, and South American writers too.

These people were books themselves, and, to them, I was a book too. I was an endless well of stories and perspectives and grand literary views. I liked the hippies a lot, because they were interested in me. When I was with them, I didn't feel judged; I felt loved. It felt so wonderful to be in their presence, like I was special.

I have never experienced a group of people who loved each other more than my hippies in the woods. All of them are tucked neatly into my memory now, and I recall our evenings discussing life and literature like a favorite film – a film I watch again when I need to be reminded about goodness, purity, and kindness.

So much of what I know about getting along with people I learned from the hippies. They were magical in community. People were drawn to them. They asked me what I loved, what I hated, and how I felt about things. What sort of music made me angry, and what sort made me sad. They asked me about my daydreams, about my favorite places in the world. They loved me like a good novel, like an art film, and this is how I felt when I was with them. Like a person John Irving would write.

I didn't feel fat or stupid or sloppily dressed. I didn't feel like I didn't know the Bible well enough or worry that I sounded immature when I talked. I had always been so conscious of things like that, but, living with the hippies, I lost my self-consciousness – and gained so much more. I gained an interest in people. I couldn't hear enough about Eddie's ballerina girlfriend or Owen's epic poems. I would ask the hippies to repeat stories, because to me they were like great scenes from my favorite movies.

Because I grew up in the safe cocoon of big-Christianity, I came to believe that anything outside the church was filled with darkness and unlove. I remember one Sunday evening: I was a child sitting in the pew, listening to the pastor read from newspaper articles – stories of burglaries, rapes, and gory murders. After each article, he would sigh and say, "Friends, it is a bad, bad world out there. And things are only getting worse."

Never in my wildest dreams would I have imagined that, outside the church, lived people so purely lovely as the ones I met in the woods. And yet my hippie friends were not at all close to believing that Christ was the Son of God. This didn't confuse me so much as it surprised me. Until I encountered the hippies, most of my friends had been Christians. And I had known love within the church. But the affection I experienced with my hippie friends seemed, well, authentic, compared to what I had known in church.

I found myself preferring the company of the hippies to the company of Christians. It wasn't that I didn't love my Christian friends or that they didn't love me; it was just that there was something different about my new friends, something more real, more true. I felt like I could be myself around the hippies. I could not be myself with my Christian friends. My Christian communities always had unwritten social rules – don't cuss, don't support Democrats, and don't ask tough questions about the Bible.

I ended up staying in the woods only a month. I wanted to stay longer. And even though I spent only a short time with the hippies, it seemed a lifetime. I learned more about people, about community, and about happiness by living in the woods than I had in a lifetime of studying those ideas philosophically.

o o o

"I THINK THE MOST IMPORTANT THING THAT HAPPENS WITHIN CHRISTIAN SPIRITUALITY IS WHEN A PERSON FALLS IN LOVE WITH JESUS."

– DON MILLER

A guy I know named Alan went around the country asking ministry leaders questions – what they were doing, what was working, what wasn't, etc. It all sounded boring except for one visit he made to a man named Bill Bright, the president of a big ministry. Alan said Bill was a big man, full of life, who listened without shifting his eyes. Alan asked a few questions, closing with "What does Jesus mean to you?"

Bill Bright could not answer this question. He just started to cry. He sat there in his big chair at his big desk and wept.

When Alan told this story, I wondered what it was like to love Jesus that way. And I wondered, quite honestly, if Dr. Bright was nuts, or if he really knew Jesus in a personal way, so well that he could cry at the mere mention of His name. I realized that I wanted to know Jesus like that. With my heart, not just my head. I felt like that would be the key to something.

I remember the first time I had feelings for Jesus. It wasn't very long ago. I had gone to a conference on the coast with some Reed students, and the speaker was a professor at a local Bible college. He spoke mostly about the Bible, about how we should read it. He was convincing. He seemed to have an emotional relationship with the Book, the way I think about *The Catcher in the Rye*. The professor reads through the Bible three times a year. I had never read through the Bible even once. I had read a lot of it, but not all of it. And I read it mainly because I felt like I had to, like it was part of a spiritual regimen.

Anyway, the speaker asked us to go outside and find a quiet place and get reacquainted with the Bible. Hold it in our hands, let our eyes feel down the pages. I went to the steps outside a rest room and opened to the book of James.

Years ago, I had a crush on a girl, so I prayed about it. And one night I read through James, because it's a book about faith and belief, and I felt like God was saying that if I had faith, this girl would marry me.

So I got very excited and lost a lot of weight. But then the girl gave her virginity to a jerk from our youth group. They're married now. I didn't care, honestly. I didn't love her that much.

But when I look at the Bible I used at the conference, I see that the book of James is highlighted in about ten colors, with words underlined all over the place. And these pages remind me of a day when I believed so faithfully in God, so beautifully in God.

That day at the conference, I read James a little, maybe a few pages. Then I shut the book, very tired and confused.

When I returned home, I felt like my Bible was calling me. I felt this promise that if I read it like a book, from cover to cover, it wouldn't change me into a clone of Pat Buchanan or something – and that, honestly, is what worried me about the Bible. So I started in Matthew. I read through Matthew and Mark, then Luke and John. I read those books in a week or so, and Jesus was very confusing. I didn't know if I liked Him very much. By the second day, I was already tired of Him.

But when I got to the end of Luke, to the part where they are going to kill Jesus, stretch Him out on a cross, something shifted within me. I remember that it was cold outside. The leaves on the trees in the park across the street were growing tired and dry. I remember sitting at my desk and feeling a love for Jesus rush through me, through my back and into my chest. I started crying, like that guy Bill Bright.

I recall thinking I would follow Jesus anywhere, that it didn't matter what he asked me to do. He could be mean to me; it didn't matter. I loved Him, and I was going to follow Him. I think the most important thing that happens within Christian spirituality is when a person falls in love with Jesus.

Sometimes when I take communion at church, take the bread and dip it in the wine, the thought of Jesus comes to me. The red of His blood or the smell of His humanity. And I eat the bread and wonder at the mystery of what I am doing – that I am somehow one with Christ, that I get my very life from Him. My spiritual life comes from His working inside of me.

I know that our culture will sometimes see a love for Jesus as a weakness. This lie floats around, which says I am supposed to be able to do life alone, without stopping to worship or serve something bigger than myself.

But I truly believe that there is something bigger than I am – and I need that. I need someone to put awe inside of me. I need to come in second to someone who has everything figured out.

All great characters in stories are the ones who give their lives to something bigger than themselves. And in all of the stories, I don't find anyone more noble than Jesus. He gave His life for me. I truly love Him for it.

I feel this love, and so do Laura, Penny, Rick, and Tony the Beat Poet. I think the difference in my life came when I realized, after reading the Gospels, that Jesus didn't just love me on principle; He didn't love me because it was the right thing to do. Rather, something inside of me caused Him to love me.

I know that if I walked up to His campfire, He would ask me to sit down, and He would ask me my story. He would listen to my ramblings or my anger until I calmed down. Then He would look me directly in the eyes, and He would speak to me. He could tell me the truth, and I would sense in his voice and in the lines on His face that he liked me. Sure, He would rebuke me, too. Tell me I hold prejudice against very religious people, and I need to deal with that. He would tell me that there are poor people in the world I need to feed, and somehow doing this will make me happy. I think He would tell me what my gifts are and why I have them and how I can use them. I think He would explain to me why my father left, and He would point out all the ways God has taken care of me and protected me through the years.

o   o   o

When I got Laura's email telling me she'd become a Christian, I just about lost it with excitement. I felt like a South African the day they let Mandela out of prison. I called her and asked her to coffee at Palio. I picked her up at Reed, and she was smiling and full of energy. She said we had very much to talk about.

At Palio, we sat in a booth in the back, and even though Laura had been my close friend, I felt I had never met her. She squirmed in her seat as she talked with confidence of her love for Jesus. I sat there amazed, because it is true. People do come to know Jesus. This crazy thing really happens. It isn't just me.

I was watching BET one night, and they were interviewing a man about jazz music. He said jazz music was invented by the first generation of out slavery. I thought that was beautiful, because, while jazz is music, it is hard to put on paper. It is a language of the soul. It's as if the soul is saying something, something about freedom. Christian spirituality is like jazz. Loving Jesus is something you feel – something very difficult to get on paper. But it is no less real, no less meaningful, no less beautiful.

The first generation out of slavery invented jazz music. It is a music birthed out of freedom. And jazz is the closest thing I know to Christian spirituality. We sing our song the way we feel it; we close our eyes and lift up our hands.

o o o

I want Jesus to happen to you the way He happened to Laura at Reed, the way He happened to me as I read the Gospels. I want you to know Jesus too. This book is about the songs my friends and I are singing. This is what God is doing in our lives. But what song will you sing when your soul gets set free? I think it will be something true and beautiful. If you haven't done it in a while, pray and talk to Jesus. Ask Him to become real to you. Ask Him to forgive you of self-addiction. Ask Him to put a song in your heart. I can't think of anything better that could happen to you than this. Much love to you, and thanks for listening to us sing.

FIVE YEARS AFTER *BLUE LIKE JAZZ*
WAS FIRST PUBLISHED,
DON MILLER REFLECTS ON
THE BLJ PHENOMENON,
TALKS ABOUT HIS NEXT BOOK,
AND REVEALS WHAT'S HAPPENING
WITH *BLUE LIKE JAZZ: THE MOVIE.*

A LOT OF PEOPLE HAVE TOLD ME HOW *BLUE LIKE JAZZ* HAS CHANGED THEIR LIVES; IT'S CHANGED MINE TOO. The way people have responded to the book has helped me feel affirmed in my message about faith. As I read the letters and emails, and meet people who have found themselves in the pages of the book, I see that I'm not the only one who feels the way I do about life. Confidence has come from that. The whole experience has been very rewarding.

And the success of *Blue Like Jazz* has given me the opportunity to continue to hone my craft. To get things right as I try to give voice to the way my generation feels about life and faith.

THE SUCCESS OF THE BOOK SURPRISED ME. I never anticipated being a voice to my generation, a voice to people in general. I just set out to be honest about my doubts about faith, to be honest about taboo subjects. I felt some people would read the book and say, "This is me, too," but I didn't know that very different people would have a similar response. I've heard from believers and non-believers, young and old.

I KNEW I WOULD GET SOME NEGATIVE FEEDBACK ON *BLUE LIKE JAZZ*. But, honestly, I anticipated about 90 percent more than I got. Maybe there's some stuff that I don't hear, but very few people are writing me with bad things to say.

IMAGO DEI, THE CHURCH I WRITE ABOUT IN THE BOOK, IS A PLACE PEOPLE CALL HOME. It's the place I call home. The church was brand-new when I was writing the book; now it's not. So there is a certain nostalgia to the way we are captured in the book.

People wonder if Pastor Rick (the church's Lead Pastor) refers to *Blue Like Jazz*, or to me, in his sermons. That doesn't happen very often. I know that we attract visitors because they've read the book – and that's neat – but Imago doesn't focus on a person. We take great care not to overemphasize any one member.

I GET A LOT OF QUESTIONS ABOUT THE PEOPLE FROM THE BOOK, BUT I DON'T LIKE TO TALK ABOUT THEM TOO MUCH. When I was writing the book, none of the people involved knew our names would become widely known. We didn't anticipate the popularity that comes with being part of a best-selling book. To us, the book is more like a snapshot of a time in our lives. It's become a bonding thing for us, and I want to protect that.

I want to avoid having my friends labeled. Tony, for example, is fond of the Tony the Beat Poet moniker and the way he is portrayed in the book. But the whole thing – people coming up and saying "Hey, Tony the Beat Poet!" – could get annoying after a while.

People who want to know more about Pastor Rick can read his blog from the Imago Web site (imagodeicommunity.com). Beyond that, I'll just say that Penny is now working for World Vision (a child-development and relief organization), and Laura is getting married, and leave it at that.

YES, *BLUE LIKE JAZZ* IS BECOMING A MOVIE. Steve Taylor, Ben Pearson, and I worked for about a year on the script. Sometimes I'd fly to Nashville to sit around a table for a week at a time and hash out the story. Sometimes Steve and Ben would come to Portland and stay at my house. Studios like Sony and Lionsgate have gotten excited about the screenplay, so we're hopeful to find a home for the movie.

As this book goes to press, we're in the process of casting so that filming can be completed, we hope, by May of 2008. We are really focused on getting things on film before the rumored Screen Actors Guild strike in a show of solidarity with the writers. Steve will direct, and I'll have some on-set responsibilities. I don't know what those are yet, though.

I don't know if I've ever had more fun – or been more challenged – by a writing project. It was a fun process to work with a team, rather than on my own. With a book, for example, I might write a paragraph that I think is funny. But then I come back to it a month later and realize it's not funny. I'll ask myself, "What kind of a mood were you in when you wrote *that*?"

But with the movie script, I would say, "Wouldn't it be funny if . . ." and Ben or Steve would explain why that wouldn't work on-screen. That kind of thing saves you a month of work. Steve is truly great at story itself – translating ideas into action and continually answering the question, "What needs to happen next?" That is not my strength. The guys really looked to me to develop the characters and create the dialogue. Ben and Steve have valued my input, and haven't become annoyed by me. At least not yet.

I really fell right into the process with Ben and Steve. I never felt like I had to make a transition to a new writing methodology. And I really like the stuff we've created.

BLUE LIKE JAZZ: THE MOVIE WILL BE A LOT DIFFERENT FROM THE BOOK. Anyone who's read the book knows how difficult it would be to turn into a movie. So we took creative liberties, gave the book a Hollywood treatment. Essentially, we took the book's major characters and gave each of them a story. Much of the movie is fictionalized, but I've shown the script to a lot of fans of the book – and, to a person, each says the script captures what the book is really about. At its core, the book reflects an idea, has a certain feel to it. The movie will do the same thing. Like the book, the film will be fun, provocative, and tender. It's really quite moving. I can't wait for people to see it.

The movie will be shot here in Portland. I am as excited about showing off my town as I am about telling the story. And some of the filming will take place at Reed College, which was such a big part of the book. It's one way for me to say thank you to the school.

THERE WILL BE ANOTHER BOOK TOO. The working title is *Story*, and it will explore why some people's lives make sense, while others' don't. My premise is that the same principles that screenwriters and novelists use to create great stories also work in creating great lives. This is a theme I touched on in *Blue Like Jazz*.

Story is not a Christian book, necessarily, with a Christian agenda. It's just about putting into practice principles that will make our own lives become better stories. It's been fun to write, and it should be out sometime in 2008.

SUCCESS DOES BRING PRESSURE. Having a best-selling book heightens expectations, but I like what that produces – better and better writing. It's nice when you read your newer stuff – then compare it with earlier work – and realize you're growing as a writer.

MY CREATIVE PROCESS HAS CHANGED WITH EACH BOOK. I wrote a lot of *Blue Like Jazz* in coffee shops around Portland. With *To Own a Dragon*, I went off to an island by myself. With *Story*, I became Office Hours Guy. It was more like a job, 9 to 5, and I liked that. There was more structure to the process, and I approached writing as a discipline. That might not sound as romantic as getting away from the office and waiting for inspiration to come, but that kind of approach is hit or miss. Some writers say, "I *need* inspiration," but inspiration will take you only half-way, at best.

WILL THERE BE ANOTHER BOOK AFTER *STORY*? I don't know. I am not the kind of writer who has 50 books in me. Only when I finish one book does a new one start to take shape. And I approach each writing project thinking, *This book could be my last one. It wouldn't surprise me at all.* But I'll always write something; it just might not be books.

MY LIFE IS NOT AS CRAZY AS IT USED TO BE. For a while, I found myself so busy – with travel and other demands – that things were spiraling out of control. But that is not happening anymore. There is more structure in my life. I am working every day, but I don't work any harder than the average businessperson. And in any average 30-day period, I am home 20 of those days. There is still the challenge, though, that the people I want to stay close to assume I don't have the time, while strangers assume that I do.

IF I COULD SAY ONE THING TO ALL THE READERS OF *BLUE LIKE JAZZ*, IT WOULD BE THANK YOU. Thank you for taking the book's message to heart. We are not in this journey alone. God really does love us. His grace toward us has become more and more true to me since the book was first published. That is what I want others to experience too.

I know that some people still struggle. They can't forgive, or won't forgive, so they don't believe God forgives them. But if we'll turn and forgive others, rather than hold grudges, we'll see how freeing that can be. And we'll understand and value God's forgiveness. So don't question your ability to forgive; just forgive.

It's the same with grace. Grace is real, and if we'll *show* grace in our lives, we'll understand and appreciate the grace that God shows to each one of us, every day.

JAZZ NOTES IS A CREATIVE REMIX

OF DONALD MILLER'S CONTEMPORARY

CLASSIC *BLUE LIKE JAZZ.*